THE OFFICIAL
Champions
League
ANNUAL 2010

Written by Pete Oliver

GRANADA

Ventures

The ITV Sport logo is licensed by Granada Ventures Ltd.

All rights reserved.

A Grange Publication

© 2009. Published by Grange Communications Ltd., Edinburgh, under licence from Granada Ventures Ltd. Printed in the EU.

Photographs © Press Association Images

ISBN 978-1-906211-75-2

£6.99

4

CONTENTS

Introduction

The 2008/09 UEFA Champions League saw another all-out assault on European glory from the cream of English football.

But despite the magnificent efforts of Chelsea, Arsenal and defending champions Manchester United in making it a hat-trick of Premier League teams to reach the semi-finals, the ultimate glory went to Spain and brilliant Barcelona.

ITV Sport were there every step of the way, bringing you the best of the action all the way to the dramatic final in Rome where Barça ended United's dreams of becoming the first club to retain the trophy in the Champions League era.

ITV Sport brought you all the twists and turns of the best club competition in the world – just like The Official ITV Sport Champions League Annual 2010 – through the highest quality words and pictures.

We also screened the final chapter of the historic UEFA Cup before it took on its new guise as the Europa Cup. The Official ITV Sport Champions League Annual 2010 retells that tale and plots the British challenge to conquer Europe again.

We never missed a kick and neither should you with this fantastic book which revives magical memories and whets the appetite for the battles to come between the best players and teams in the world.

Enjoy it with us.

itv SPORT

Brilliant Barça

BARCELONA were crowned kings of Europe for the third time in their history as they overcame holders Manchester United on a magical night in Rome.

Goals from Samuel Eto'o and Lionel Messi gave the Spanish giants a deserved 2-0 win in a triumphant Champions League final.

Premier League and World Club champions Manchester United were just no match for Pep Guardiola's men, who completed their own unique treble after also winning the La Liga title and the Spanish Cup.

"What we have done is historic, this is fantastic," said Eto'o, whose early goal was key to victory.

"The whole team played fantastic, from Xavi to Iniesta. It's been a great team effort from the start of the season."

After United had started well in the Stadio Olimpico they were rocked when Eto'o cut inside Nemanja Vidic and beat Edwin van der Sar at his near post.

From then United were chasing the game and with Barcelona proving masters of possession, highlighted by the magnificent Andres Iniesta, Sir Alex Ferguson's men could not get enough of the ball to create any sustained pressure.

And they were killed off completely mid-way through the second half when Xavi's beautiful cross was headed in by Messi to sum up brilliant Barça.

MESSI
MAGIC

LITTLE genius Lionel Messi could not have chosen a more fitting way to cap a memorable season than by scoring the clinching goal in the 2009 Champions League final.

The mesmeric Messi played a massive part in helping Barcelona become the first Spanish club to win the treble of La Liga, Spanish Cup and the Champions League.

The Argentina international bagged a staggering 38 goals as defenders were left in his wake right across Europe.

Officially the second best player on the planet behind Manchester United's Cristiano Ronaldo, Messi upset the rankings with a stellar performance against United in the European final in Rome.

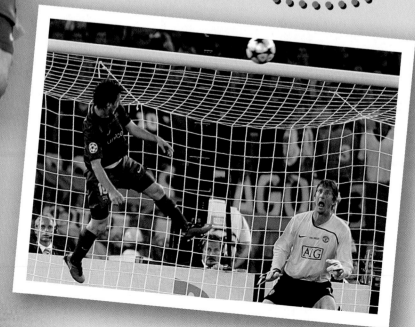

Usually famous for his quick feet and dazzling dribbling, this time the diminutive forward did the damage with his head as he nodded in a cross from Xavi to complete Barcelona's 2-0 win and – for one night at least – put himself on top of the footballing world.

Messi said: "To score in a Champions League final against Manchester United and win the League title is just unbelievable. It's a dream. This has been an unbelievable season.

"I think it will take us a long time to realise what we have achieved."

Tears by the Tiber

MANCHESTER United's dreams of becoming the first team to successfully defend the Champions League title since the competition evolved from the European Cup were shattered in Rome.

United's superb run to the final, which saw them overwhelm Arsenal in the last four after remaining unbeaten through the group and knock-out stages, gave them the chance of an unprecedented haul of four trophies when they took on Barcelona in the Stadio Olimpico.

But after winning the Premier League, Carling Cup and World Club Cup, Sir Alex Ferguson's men found the Champions League final one game too far.

Cristiano Ronaldo almost scored with a scorching early free-kick and also sent another shot skidding just wide in his last game for the club before his world record move to Real Madrid.

But Samuel Eto'o rocked United when he counter-attacked to put Barça ahead after ten minutes.

United had shown great character to negotiate a tricky quarter-final tie against Porto when

they needed a goal from Ronaldo in his native Portugal to progress.

And again they dug deep to launch a brief second-half fightback in Rome as club legend Ryan Giggs came close to an equaliser.

But their hopes were finally snuffed out when Lionel Messi made sure the trophy would head to Spain when his towering header made it 2-0.

So like Chelsea 12 months earlier, this time it was United's turn to feel the heartache as their haul of European crowns was left at three.

"It is a big disappointment but Barcelona were the better team," admitted United forward Wayne Rooney.

"Barcelona are a brilliant team and in my opinion Andres Iniesta is the best player in the world."

Barcelona are certainly on top of the world but the famous hunger of United and their manager means they will be back challenging again in 2010.

"We have to forget it and look forward to next time," Rooney added.

The rest have been warned.

PEP TALK

BARCELONA boss Josep "Pep" Guardiola joined an elite band of football greats when he led the Catalans to Champions League glory against Manchester United.

Barça's 2-0 triumph in the final in Rome meant Guardiola became one of only six men to have won the European crown as a player and a coach.

The Nou Camp legend was part of the Barcelona team that won the competition in its final year as the European Cup in 1992 when they beat Italian club Sampdoria at Wembley.

And the former Spanish international midfielder then master-minded the club's third success in the tournament, joining former Barcelona managers Johan Cruyff and Frank Rijkaard in the hall of fame, when they got the better of United in the Stadio Olimpico.

Remarkably the success came in Guardiola's first season as coach, which also saw Barça win their domestic league and cup titles to claim the treble for the first time in a blitz of magnificent attacking football.

Guardiola had previously spent 12 months as Barcelona's 'B' team coach before being promoted to replace Rijkaard in an inspired decision by the Catalan club as Barça regained their title as kings of Europe for the first time since 2006.

"We're aware that we've done something magnificent. I'd like to congratulate the whole club and the fans," said Guardiola.

"We're not the best team in Barça history but we've had the best season. We've won three trophies but it's also about how we've won them."

SIX OF THE BEST

The six men who have won the Champions League or European Cup as a player and coach are: Pep Guardiola, Frank Rijkaard, Johan Cruyff, Carlo Ancelotti, Miguel Muñoz and Giovanni Trapattoni.

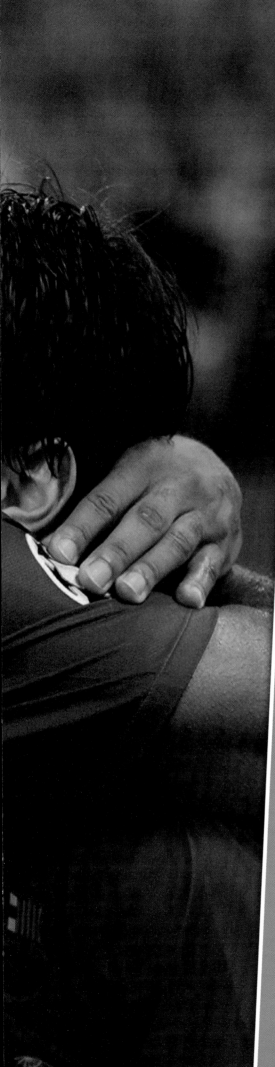

How the Cup was Won

Champions League Final 2009

May 27
Stadio Olimpico, Rome, Italy
Kick-off 7.45BST

Barcelona 2
(Eto'o 10mins, Messi 70mins)
Manchester United 0

Barcelona: Valdes, Puyol, Toure Yaya, Pique, Sylvinho, Xavi, Busquets, Iniesta (Pedrito 90), Messi, Eto'o, Henry (Keita 72).
Subs Not Used: Pinto, Caceres, Muniesa, Gudjohnsen, Bojan.

Booked: Pique.

Manchester Utd: Van der Sar, O'Shea, Ferdinand, Vidic, Evra, Anderson (Tevez 46), Carrick, Giggs (Scholes 75), Park (Berbatov 66), Ronaldo, Rooney.
Subs Not Used: Kuszczak, Rafael Da Silva, Evans, Nani.

Booked: Ronaldo, Scholes, Vidic.

Attendance: 72,700

Referee: Massimo Busacca (Switzerland).

All Roads Lead to Rome

GROUP RESULTS 2008/09

Matchday 1 - Tuesday 16 September

Grp	Home		Away
A	Chelsea	4-0	Bordeaux
A	Roma	1-2	CFR Cluj
B	Panathinaikos	0-2	Internazionale
B	Bremen	0-0	Anorthosis
C	Basel	1-2	Shakhtar
C	Barcelona	3-1	Sporting
D	PSV	0-3	Atlético
D	Marseille	1-2	Liverpool

Matchday 1 - Wednesday 17 September

Grp	Home		Away
E	Man. United	0-0	Villarreal
E	Celtic	0-0	AaB
F	Steaua	0-1	Bayern
F	Lyon	2-2	Fiorentina
G	Porto	3-1	Fenerbahçe
G	Dynamo Kiev	1-1	Arsenal
H	Juventus	1-0	Zenit
H	Real Madrid	2-0	BATE

Matchday 2 - Tuesday 30 September

Grp	Home		Away
E	AaB	0-3	Man. United
E	Villarreal	1-0	Celtic
F	Fiorentina	0-0	Steaua
F	Bayern	1-1	Lyon
G	Arsenal	4-0	Porto
G	Fenerbahçe	0-0	Dynamo Kiev
H	BATE	2-2	Juventus
H	Zenit	1-2	Real Madrid

Matchday 2 - Wednesday 1 October

Grp	Home		Away
A	CFR Cluj	0-0	Chelsea
A	Bordeaux	1-3	Roma
B	Anorthosis	3-1	Panathinaikos
B	Internazionale	1-1	Bremen
C	Sporting	2-0	Basel
C	Shakhtar	1-2	Barcelona
D	Liverpool	3-1	PSV
D	Atlético	2-1	Marseille

Matchday 3 - Tuesday 21 October

Grp	Home		Away
E	Villarreal	6-3	AaB
E	Man. United	3-0	Celtic
F	Bayern	3-0	Fiorentina
F	Steaua	3-5	Lyon
G	Fenerbahçe	2-5	Arsenal
G	Porto	0-1	Dynamo Kiev
H	Zenit	1-1	BATE
H	Juventus	2-1	Real Madrid

Matchday 3 - Wednesday 22 October

Grp	Home		Away
A	Bordeaux	1-0	CFR Cluj
A	Chelsea	1-0	Roma
B	Internazionale	1-0	Anorthosis
B	Panathinaikos	2-2	Bremen
C	Shakhtar	0-1	Sporting
C	Basel	0-5	Barcelona
D	Atlético	1-1	Liverpool
D	PSV	2-0	Marseille

Matchday 4 - Tuesday 4 November

Grp	Home		Away
A	CFR Cluj	1-2	Bordeaux
A	Roma	3-1	Chelsea
B	Anorthosis	3-3	Internazionale
B	Bremen	0-3	Panathinaikos
C	Sporting	1-0	Shakhtar
C	Barcelona	1-1	Basel
D	Liverpool	1-1	Atlético
D	Marseille	3-0	PSV

Matchday 4 - Wednesday 5 November

Grp	Home		Away
E	AaB	2-2	Villarreal
E	Celtic	1-1	Man. United
F	Fiorentina	1-1	Bayern
F	Lyon	2-0	Steaua
G	Arsenal	0-0	Fenerbahçe
G	Dynamo Kiev	1-2	Porto
H	BATE	0-2	Zenit
H	Real Madrid	0-2	Juventus

Matchday 5 - Tuesday 25 November

Grp	Home		Away
E	Villarreal	0-0	Man. United
E	AaB	2-1	Celtic
F	Bayern	3-0	Steaua
F	Fiorentina	1-2	Lyon
G	Fenerbahçe	1-2	Porto
G	Arsenal	1-0	Dynamo Kiev
H	Zenit	0-0	Juventus
H	BATE	0-1	Real Madrid

Matchday 5 - Wednesday 26 November

Grp	Home		Away
A	Bordeaux	1-1	Chelsea
A	CFR Cluj	1-3	Roma
B	Internazionale	0-1	Panathinaikos
B	Anorthosis	2-2	Bremen
C	Shakhtar	5-0	Basel
C	Sporting	2-5	Barcelona
D	Atlético	2-1	PSV
D	Liverpool	1-0	Marseille

Matchday 6 - Tuesday 9 December

Grp	Home		Away
A	Chelsea	2-1	CFR Cluj
A	Roma	2-0	Bordeaux
B	Panathinaikos	1-0	Anorthosis
B	Bremen	2-1	Internazionale
C	Basel	0-1	Sporting
C	Barcelona	2-3	Shakhtar
D	PSV	1-3	Liverpool
D	Marseille	0-0	Atlético

Matchday 6 - Wednesday 10 December

Grp	Home		Away
E	Man. United	2-2	AaB
E	Celtic	2-0	Villarreal
F	Steaua	0-1	Fiorentina
F	Lyon	2-3	Bayern
G	Porto	2-0	Arsenal
G	Dynamo Kiev	1-0	Fenerbahçe
H	Juventus	0-0	BATE
H	Real Madrid	3-0	Zenit

All Roads Lead to Rome

GROUP RESULTS 2008/09

GROUP A

	P	W	D	L	F	A	P
AS Roma	6	4	0	2	12	6	12
Chelsea	6	3	2	1	9	5	11
Bordeaux	6	2	1	3	5	11	7
CFR-Cluj	6	1	1	4	5	9	4

GROUP B

	P	W	D	L	F	A	P
Panathinaikos	6	3	1	2	8	7	10
Internazionale	6	2	2	2	8	7	8
Werder Bremen	6	1	4	1	7	9	7
Anorthosis	6	1	3	2	8	8	6

GROUP C

	P	W	D	L	F	A	P
Barcelona	6	4	1	1	18	8	13
Sporting Lisbon	6	4	0	2	8	8	12
Shakhtar Donetsk	6	3	0	3	11	7	9
Basel	6	0	1	5	2	16	1

GROUP D

	P	W	D	L	F	A	P
Liverpool	6	4	2	0	11	5	14
Atlético Madrid	6	3	3	0	9	4	12
Marseille	6	1	1	4	5	7	4
PSV Eindhoven	6	1	0	5	5	14	3

GROUP E

	P	W	D	L	F	A	P
Man Utd	6	2	4	0	9	3	10
Villarreal	6	2	3	1	9	7	9
AaB Aalborg	6	1	3	2	9	14	6
Celtic	6	1	2	3	4	7	5

GROUP F

	P	W	D	L	F	A	P
Bayern Munich	6	4	2	0	12	4	14
Lyon	6	3	2	1	14	10	11
Fiorentina	6	1	3	2	5	8	6
Steaua Bucharest	6	0	1	5	3	12	1

GROUP G

	P	W	D	L	F	A	P
Porto	6	4	0	2	9	8	12
Arsenal	6	3	2	1	11	5	11
Dynamo Kiev	6	2	2	2	4	4	8
Fenerbahçe	6	0	2	4	4	11	2

GROUP H

	P	W	D	L	F	A	P
Juventus	6	3	3	0	7	3	12
Real Madrid	6	4	0	2	9	5	12
Zenit St. Petersburg	6	1	2	3	4	7	5
BATE Borisov	6	0	3	3	3	8	3

All Roads Lead

FIRST KNOCKOUT ROUND

Team			
Lyon	1	2	**3**
Barcelona	1	5	**6**

Team			
Sporting CP	0	1	**1**
Bayern Munich	5	7	**12**

Team			
Real Madrid	0	0	**0**
Liverpool	1	4	**5**

Team			
Chelsea	1	2	**3**
Juventus	0	2	**2**

Team			
Internazionale	0	0	**0**
Manchester United	0	2	**2**

Team			
Atlético Madrid	2	0	**2**
Porto (a)	2	0	**2**

Team			
Villarreal	1	2	**3**
Panathinaikos	1	1	**2**

Team			
Arsenal (p)	1	0	**1(7)**
Roma	0	1	**1(6)**

QUARTER-FINALS

Barcelona	4	1	**5**
Bayern Munich	0	1	**1**

Team			
Liverpool	1	4	**5**
Chelsea	3	4	**7**

Team			
Manchester United	2	1	**3**
Porto	2	0	**2**

Team			
Villarreal	1	0	**1**
Arsenal	1	3	**4**

to Rome

SEMI-FINALS	FINAL

🇪🇸 **Barcelona**		**2**
✠ Manchester United		**0**

🇪🇸 **Barcelona (a)**	0	1	**1**
✠ Chelsea	0	1	**1**

✠ **Manchester United**	1	3	**4**
✠ Arsenal	0	1	**1**

Rome Hails The Champions

ROME'S Stadio Olimpico proved a fitting venue to hail Barcelona as the new kings of Europe.

Barça against Manchester United was a true battle of the gladiators where Lionel Messi outshone Cristiano Ronaldo to take the Champions League trophy back to Spain.

"There was no duel. Barcelona were better on the night," admitted Ronaldo after United had lost 2-0.

The magnificent stadium in Italy's capital had twice before hosted English success in the European Cup.

Liverpool were crowned as champions in Rome in 1977 and 1984 before Juventus also tasted European glory at the Stadio Olimpico as Champions League winners in 1996.

ROMA
FINALE 2009

The historic stadium staged its first events in 1938 before being refurbished for a second opening in 1953.

It then hosted the Olympic Games in 1960 and the World Cup final in 1990 when West Germany beat Argentina in the final.

Madrid's Bernabeu Stadium will host the 2010 Champions League final and has a lot to live up to.

Champions League Quiz

Test your knowledge of the Champions League with this fun quiz

 1 Barcelona striker Samuel Eto'o plays for which country?

 2 How many times have Barcelona won the Champions League and European Cup?

 3 Who was the Chelsea manager who guided the Blues to the semi-finals of the 2008/09 Champions League?

 4 Where will the 2010 Champions League final be played?

 5 Which club has played in the most Champions League finals?

 6 CFR Cluj were the surprise package of the 2008/09 Champions League. Which country do they come from?

 7 Which Manchester United player missed the 2008/09 Champions League final through suspension?

 8 What was the aggregate score when Chelsea knocked Liverpool out in the quarter-finals of the 2008/09 Champions League?

 9 Which is the only Scottish club to have won the European Cup?

 10 Who was Liverpool's leading scorer in the 2008/09 Champions League?

 11 Who beat Arsenal in the final of the Champions League in 2006?

 12 Who is the captain of Barcelona who lifted the 2008/09 Champions League trophy in Rome?

Answers on page 61

GOAL-DEN BOYS

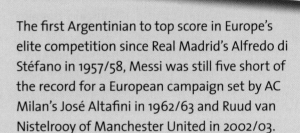

BARCELONA superstar Lionel Messi stamped his mark all over the 2008/09 Champions League so it was no surprise to see the little magician top the scoring charts.

Of Messi's 38 goals during a historic season for the Catalan club, nine came in the Champions League – including the second goal in Barça's 2-0 final win over Manchester United.

A towering header past a bemused Edwin van dar Sar proved that despite standing at little more than five-and-a-half feet tall, the Argentinian international has every possible weapon in his armoury.

Messi finished two clear of Liverpool's Steven Gerrard, who again underlined his remarkable goal-scoring record as an attacking midfielder, and Bayern Munich's German international Miroslav Klose.

The first Argentinian to top score in Europe's elite competition since Real Madrid's Alfredo di Stéfano in 1957/58, Messi was still five short of the record for a European campaign set by AC Milan's José Altafini in 1962/63 and Ruud van Nistelrooy of Manchester United in 2002/03.

United's lack of an out-and-out goalscorer in 2008/09 saw them share the workload in front of goal as Chelsea's Didier Drogba and the Arsenal pair of Robin van Persie and Emmanuel Adebayor continued the chase from the British clubs with five each.

Lionel Messi	**9**	**Barcelona**
Steven Gerrard	**7**	**Liverpool**
Miroslav Klose	**7**	**Bayern**
Lisandro	**6**	**Porto**
Emmanuel Adebayor	**5**	**Arsenal**
Alessandro Del Piero	**5**	**Juventus**
Didier Drogba	**5**	**Chelsea**
Robin van Persie	**5**	**Arsenal**
Thierry Henry	**5**	**Barcelona**
Karim Benzema	**5**	**Lyon**
Jadson	**4**	**Shakhtar**
Danny Koevermans	**4**	**PSV**
Joseba Llorente	**4**	**Villarreal**
Dimitar Berbatov	**4**	**Man. United**
Vangelis Mantzios	**4**	**Panathinaikos**
Alberto Gilardino	**4**	**Fiorentina**
Franck Ribéry	**4**	**Bayern**
Samuel Eto'o	**4**	**Barcelona**
Wayne Rooney	**4**	**Man. United**
Cristiano Ronaldo	**4**	**Man. United**

29

Bridge of Sighs

CHELSEA'S run to the last four of the 2008/09 Champions League made it five semi-final appearances in six years in a remarkable record of consistency.

But with Barcelona dashing the Blues' hopes of a second successive final appearance in heart-breaking fashion, the Holy Grail of the Champions League title again eluded the Londoners.

So with Guus Hiddink handing over the managerial baton to Carlo Ancelotti, the weight of expectation at Stamford Bridge now falls on the shoulders of the Italian who has previously won the European crown as a player and manager of AC Milan. Can he now work his magic at Chelsea?

After losing the 2008 final to Manchester United on penalties it was again a case of so near, yet so far for Chelsea in 2009.

Under the charge of Brazilian Luiz Felipe Scolari, the Blues stuttered their way through qualification with defeats at Roma and a goalless draw away to CFR Cluj before victory in their final game against the Romanian minnows secured second place in Group A.

By the time of the knock-out stages, Hiddink had been installed as manager on a temporary basis and the Dutchman got his first win in a 1-0 first-leg victory over Juventus thanks to a Didier Drogba goal.

Former Chelsea manager Claudio Ranieri made sure that Juventus would not go down without a fight but goals from Michael Essien and Drogba earned a 2-2 draw in the second leg in Italy, ensuring Chelsea's further progress in the competition.

Once again Liverpool stood in Chelsea's path in the quarter-finals but there would be no stopping the Blues as they triumphed in an epic clash.

In four previous trips to Anfield in the competition Chelsea had only scored once thanks to a John Arne Riise own-goal 12 months previously.

When Fernando Torres scored early on it looked as though the trend may continue but two headed goals from defender Branislav Ivanovic, his first for the club, and another from Drogba gave Chelsea a 3-1 advantage to take back to the Bridge.

Any thoughts of an easy passage were soon dismissed, though, as rampant Liverpool surged into a 2-0 lead through Fabio Aurelio and a Xabi Alonso penalty to level the scores.

Stirred into action Chelsea hit back through Drogba, Alex's thunderbolt and Frank Lampard but still Liverpool were not finished as Lucas, with a deflected shot, and Dirk Kuyt put the Reds within a goal of pulling off a remarkable win.

The force might have been with Liverpool but once again Lampard proved Chelsea's saviour as he swept home the equaliser to take Chelsea through 7-5 to meet Barcelona in the semi-finals.

A goalless draw in the first leg at Nou Camp looked to have given the Blues the edge as they produced a highly disciplined performance to stifle the threat of Barça's big guns.

But the drama was to come in the second leg as Chelsea cruelly had a place in the final in Rome snatched away from them right at the death.

On a controversial night when Chelsea thought they should have been awarded a couple of penalties they led through Michael Essien's spectacular early strike.

But despite the dismissal of Barça defender Abidal, Hiddink's men could not find the second goal and that cost them in injury time when Andrés Iniesta scored with the Catalans' only shot on target to leave Chelsea devastated and Barcelona heading for the final and ultimate success against Manchester United.

31

ROLL OF HONOUR

Champions League/ European Cup winners

BARCELONA'S Champions League final triumph over Manchester United earned the Spanish giants their third European crown, placing them level with United.

Barça's big rivals Real Madrid still lead the way with nine titles, although it's over ten years since the trophy found its way back to the Bernabeu Stadium.

2008 – 2009 FC Barcelona

2007 – 2008 Manchester United

2006 - 2007 AC Milan

2005 - 2006 FC Barcelona

2004 - 2005 Liverpool

2003 - 2004 FC Porto

2002 - 2003 AC Milan

2001 - 2002 Real Madrid

2000 - 2001 FC Bayern München

1999 - 2000 Real Madrid

1998 - 1999 Manchester United

1997 - 1998 Real Madrid

1996 - 1997 BV Borussia Dortmund

1995 - 1996 Juventus

1994 - 1995 AFC Ajax

1993 - 1994 AC Milan

1992 - 1993 Olympique de Marseille

1991 - 1992 FC Barcelona

1990 - 1991 FK Crvena Zvezda

1989 - 1990 AC Milan

1988 - 1989 AC Milan

1987 - 1988 PSV Eindhoven

1986 - 1987 FC Porto

1985 - 1986 FC Steaua Bucuresti

1984 - 1985 Juventus

1983 - 1984 Liverpool

1982 - 1983 Hamburger SV

1981 - 1982 Aston Villa

1980 - 1981 Liverpool

1979 - 1980 Nottingham Forest

1978 - 1979 Nottingham Forest

1977 - 1978 Liverpool

1976 - 1977 Liverpool

1975 - 1976 FC Bayern München

1974 - 1975 FC Bayern München

1973 - 1974 FC Bayern München

1972 - 1973 AFC Ajax

1971 - 1972 AFC Ajax

1970 - 1971 AFC Ajax

1969 - 1970 Feyenoord

1968 - 1969 AC Milan

1967 - 1968 Manchester United

1966 - 1967 Celtic

1965 - 1966 Real Madrid

1964 - 1965 FC Internazionale Milano

1963 - 1964 FC Internazionale Milano

1962 - 1963 AC Milan

1961 - 1962 SL Benfica

1960 - 1961 SL Benfica

1959 - 1960 Real Madrid

1958 - 1959 Real Madrid

1957 - 1958 Real Madrid

1956 - 1957 Real Madrid

1955 - 1956 Real Madrid

CHAMPION CLASS

Champions League Highlights 2008/09

BARCELONA conquered Europe in 2009 but there were plenty of other winners along the way who all had their moments of glory on the road to Rome. We've picked out some of the highlights to enjoy again.

Fenerbahçe 2, Arsenal 5

TURKEY has always been a difficult place for visiting teams to go and Fenerbahçe boasted a 15-match unbeaten home record in Europe when Arsenal arrived for their Group G clash.

However, that was blown apart by a rampant Gunners team as they racked up one of their most impressive away wins in the competition.

Emmanuel Adebayor and Theo Walcott gave Arsène Wenger's men a flying start and even though Mikael Silvestre deflected into his own net Arsenal were 3-1 up mid-way through the first half when Abou Diaby scored.

Alexandre Song got the fourth and even though Fenerbahçe pulled one back through Daniel Guiza, teenage substitute Aaron Ramsey marked his competition debut with another for Arsenal as they forged on with a run that took them to the semi-finals.

Roma 1, CFR Cluj 2

ROMANIAN minnows Cluj made a stunning entry into the competition as they carved out their own piece of history in the Stadio Olimpico.

Playing their first group game in the Champions League, Cluj stunned Roma by coming from behind to earn a shock win.

When Christian Panucci scored first for the Italian giants it looked like a straightforward night for Roma.

But two goals from Argentinian midfielder Juan Culio made it a triumphant homecoming for Cluj's Italian coach Maurizio Trombetta.

Sadly, though, the fairytale didn't last as Cluj didn't win another game and finished bottom of Group A, while Roma advanced as group winners.

Anorthosis 3, Panathinaikos 1

CYPRUS had never produced a winning team in the Champions League group stages but that record was ended in memorable style by domestic title holders Anorthosis Famagusta.

Anorthosis, managed by former Newcastle United striker Temuri Ketsbaia, marked the country's Independence Day by beating Greek neighbours Panathinaikos in Nikosia to make it four points from their opening two games.

An own-goal from José Sarriegi and a Sinisa Dobrasinovic header got the party started in front of 20,000 home fans.

Dimitris Salpigidis pulled one back from the penalty spot before half-time but a header from substitute Hawar Taher gave Anorthosis the points.

Their impressive run continued by going through the group stage unbeaten at home but that was still not enough to stop them finishing bottom of Group B, while Panathinaikos recovered to go through as winners.

Liverpool 4, Real Madrid 0 (5-0 on aggregate)

LIVERPOOL stole the initiative in their last-16 tie against six-times winners Real Madrid by winning 1-0 at the Bernabeu Stadium.

And any thoughts of a nervy rearguard action in the second leg were soon dismissed on another famous European night at Anfield.

Shrugging aside their usual cautious approach, Rafa Benitez's side tore Real apart to hand the shell-shocked Spanish giants their biggest ever defeat in the Champions League as Liverpool reached the quarter-finals for the third year in a row.

Spanish superstar Fernando Torres opened the floodgates and it was one-way traffic as Steven Gerrard doubled Liverpool's lead from the penalty spot.

A stunning third from Gerrard early in the second half confirmed Real's fifth successive last-16 defeat before Andrea Dossena added the icing to the cake with a late fourth.

Bayern Munich 7, Sporting Lisbon 1 (aggregate 12-1)

BAYERN Munich re-wrote the record books with this hammering of Sporting Lisbon as the Germans racked up the biggest individual and aggregate victories in a Champions League knock-out tie.

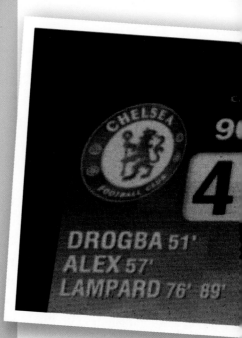

Jurgen Klinsmann's side already had one foot in the quarter-finals thanks to a 5-0 win in Portugal when they brought Sporting back to the Arena in Munich.

And despite missing star talents Franck Ribery and Luca Toni through injury, Bayern showed no mercy as they romped to an incredible 7-1 win in the second leg.

Lukas Podolski scored twice in the first half, along with Bastian Schweinsteiger and an own-goal from Anderson Polga.

Joao Moutinho momentarily stemmed the flow with arguably the goal of the game but Bayern weren't finished as they added to their tally after the break through Mark van Bommel, a Miroslav Klose penalty and a debutant goal from teenager Thomas Müller.

Barcelona 4, Bayern Munich 0 (aggregate 5-1)

IT WAS a different story for Bayern Munich in the quarter-finals when they were on the receiving end of a goal blitz from would-be champions Barcelona.

Pep Guardiola's side turned on the style in typically breath-taking fashion at the Nou Camp with four first-half goals virtually guaranteeing their place in the semi-finals.

Bayern had won all of their previous meetings at Barcelona but had no answer this time to the dazzling feet of Lionel Messi and company.

Messi scored twice and also laid one on for Samuel Eto'o before Thierry Henry netted his 50th Champions League goal in a five-star showing.

Barcelona took their foot off the pedal after the break and then strolled through the second leg with a 1-1 draw to take their place in the last four.

Chelsea 4, Liverpool 4 (aggregate 7-5)

CHELSEA duly took their place in the semi-finals for the fifth time in six years but not before they were given a major fright by Liverpool in a classic encounter at Stamford Bridge.

Liverpool looked to be down and out when they lost the first leg 3-1 at Anfield and were further handicapped for the return when inspirational captain Steven Gerrard was ruled out with injury.

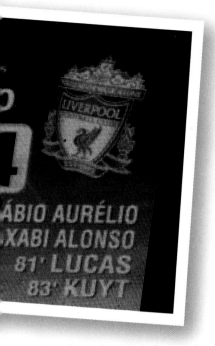

But a clever free-kick from Fabio Aurelio gave them hope and when Xabi Alonso scored from the spot the aggregate scores were level and Chelsea were rocking by half-time.

Didier Drogba replied to steady the nerves and a thunderbolt from Alex and a Frank Lampard strike looked to have killed off Liverpool's challenge.

But the Reds refused to lie down and a deflected Lucas goal and a Dirk Kuyt header put Liverpool 4-3 ahead on the night and within one goal of progressing.

Liverpool had seven minutes to try and find it but instead it was Lampard who again delivered the goods for Chelsea by sweeping home an equaliser to finally take Guus Hiddink's men through.

Arsenal 1, Manchester United 3 (aggregate 1-4)

ARSENAL 'escaped' from Old Trafford with a 1-0 defeat from their first leg of their semi-final to keep alive hopes of a first ever triumph in the Champions League.

The Gunners also had a five-year unbeaten home record to rely on as they looked to overturn the deficit and release Manchester United's grip on the trophy they won in 2008.

But instead it was Sir Alex Ferguson's men who triumphed as they produced a performance worthy of champions.

United over-powered their domestic rivals with an awesome display and never looked back once Ji-Sung Park capitalised on an early mistake to open the scoring.

Cristiano Ronaldo then blasted in a long-range free-kick before adding the third in the second-half when he rounded off a superb counter-attack.

United were on their way to Rome, apart from luckless midfielder Darren Fletcher who was sent off for bringing down Cesc Fabregas for Robin van Persie to score a consolation from the penalty spot.

Superstars of Europe

STEVEN GERRARD

WHEN it comes to the cream of Europe, homegrown talent Steven Gerrard can claim to be right up there with the best of them.

Liverpool's captain and attacking midfielder has spent all his career at Anfield and has led the Merseyside club to every major trophy bar the Premier League.

His performance in leading Liverpool's fightback to beat AC Milan in the 2005 Champions League final marked the England international down as an all-time great.

Fittingly on his 100th European appearance for the Reds, Gerrard scored twice against Real Madrid in a last-16 tie in the 2008/09 Champions League, inspiring Liverpool to an epic 4-0 win.

Not long afterwards, three times world player of the year Zinedine Zidane suggested that Gerrard deserved to take on his mantle as the best player on the planet.

PROFILE
Born: Liverpool, May 1980
Clubs: Liverpool
Position: Midfielder
International: England

FRANCK RIBERY

FRANCE has produced some outstanding midfield players down the years with Franck Ribery carrying the flag for the current generation.

After taking time to establish himself in the early part of his career, Ribery played for a handful of clubs before finding his feet with Marseille.

Emerging as a major talent, Bayern Munich paid a club record fee for his services in 2007 and in his first season in the Bundesliga, Ribery was named German footballer of the year as Bayern won the league title.

Scoring at a rate of close to a goal every two games, the France international became one of the hottest properties in the game with his pace and dazzling skill sending his value soaring.

And after helping Bayern to the quarter-finals of the 2008/09 Champions League, he was courted by the top clubs in Europe as they scrambled to try and secure his services.

PROFILE
Born: Boulogne-sur-Mer, France, April 1983
Clubs: Boulogne, Ales, Stade Brestois, Metz, Galatasaray, Marseilles, Bayern Munich
Position: Midfielder
International: France

MIROSLAV KLOSE

WHEN it comes to selecting the most efficient and consistent goalscorers in Europe, Miroslav Klose deserves to have his name firmly in the frame.

The Polish-born German international boasts a phenomenal strike-rate at both club and international level.

The first player to score five goals in successive World Cup finals, his haul in 2006 earned him the Golden Boot award as he helped the host country reach the semi-finals.

Playing all his club football in Germany, Klose scored 20 times in his first season at Bayern Munich to help secure a league and cup double in 2008.

That tally attracted envious glances from across Europe but Klose, a classical all-round striker, stayed with Bayern and scored seven times as the Germans reached the last eight of the 2008/09 Champions League.

PROFILE

Born: Opole, Poland, June 1978
Clubs: Kaiserslautern, Werder Bremen, Bayern Munich
Position: Striker
International: Germany

WAYNE ROONEY

THE 2008/09 season ended in disappointment for Wayne Rooney with Manchester United's defeat in the Champions League final against Barcelona.

But taken as a whole, the year was another triumph for the England international as he helped United to the treble of Premier League, Carling Cup and World Club Cup.

Rooney contributed 17 goals to the cause but that tells only half the story as he also played a key role as a supplier for Cristiano Ronaldo, Carlos Tevez and Dimitar Berbatov as he filled a variety of attacking roles at Old Trafford.

Since bursting onto the scene as a precocious talent at Everton, Rooney has always been marked out as an exceptional talent.

His vision, power and commitment have made him one of the outstanding players of his generation and a first name on the team sheet for both United and England with his ten goals in the 2008/09 season equalling Gary Lineker's England record and taking Fabio Capello's side to the brink of the World Cup finals.

PROFILE

Born: Liverpool, October 1985
Clubs: Everton, Manchester United
Position: Forward
International: England

TROPHY TRAIL

Solution on page 61

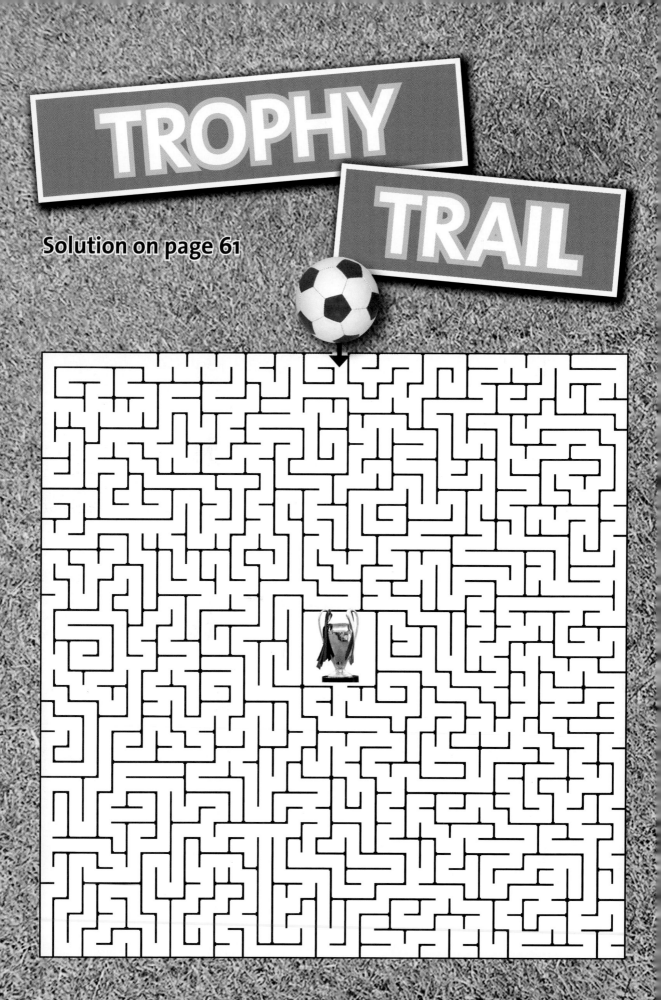

42

Great Goalies

GOALSCORERS often grab the glory but most successful teams are built on a solid back line with the goalkeeper a key component, who can influence a game just as much as any centre-forward. Here are four of the best.

VICTOR VALDES

A CLEAN sheet against Manchester United in the 2008/09 Champions League final earned Victor Valdes a second winners' medal in Europe's elite competition.

He also has three La Liga titles to his credit since becoming a permanent fixture at the Nou Camp in the 2003/04 season.

In the 2006/07 league season Valdes was an ever-present for Barça, equalling a record previously set by club legend Andoni Zubizarreta and in April 2008 he clocked up his 250th game for the club.

Valdes' reactions and shot-stopping skills have twice earned him the Zamora Trophy as the best goalkeeper in Spain.

But remarkably by the end of the 2008/09 season he had never won a senior cap for Spain due to their embarrassment of riches in the goalkeeping department.

PROFILE
Born: Barcelona, Spain January 1982
Clubs: Barcelona
International: Spain under-21

IKER CASILLAS

SPAIN'S undoubted number-one, Iker Casillas is another one-club man who has given magnificent service to Real Madrid.

A product of the club's youth set-up, Casillas graduated to the first-team in 1999 and the following year became the youngest goalkeeper to play in a Champions League final when he helped Real beat Valencia having just turned 19.

He picked up another Champions League winners' medal in 2002 when he came off the bench to produce a stunning performance against Bayer Leverkusen and has been a fixture in the first-team ever since.

Twice an ever-present during league seasons he has helped Real win four La Liga titles with his efforts in the 2007/08 success earning him the Zamora Trophy as the country's top goalkeeper.

That is also reflected in his statistics with the national team with his near 100 appearances making him Spain's second most capped goalkeeper behind Andoni Zubizarreta.

Casillas captained Spain in the 2008 European Championships when penalty shoot-out saves and clean sheets in the quarter-finals, semi-finals and final helped Spain win the tournament and see him lift the trophy in Austria.

PROFILE
Born: Madrid, Spain, May 1981
Clubs: Real Madrid
International: Spain

PETR CECH

THE IMPOSING figure of Petr Cech has been a constant in Chelsea's success story with the Londoners twice winning the Premier League, the FA Cup and the League Cup during his time at Stamford Bridge.

Cech also helped the Blues reach the final of the Champions League in 2008 and while he finished on the losing side in a penalty shoot-out his recognition as the outstanding goalkeeper in the competition for three seasons out of four from 2004 underlined his status in the game.

At six feet, five inches tall Cech has often proved an impregnable barrier with the statistics confirming that impression.

He still holds the Czech record for not conceding a goal for 855 minutes from his time at Sparta Prague and following his move to Chelsea kept 25 clean sheets as Jose Mourinho's side won the league title in 2005.

His run of 1,025 minutes without being beaten in the Premier League was also a record until Edwin van der Sar bettered it in Manchester United's title success of 2008/09.

A serious head injury which sidelined him for three months threatened to remove Cech's air of invincibility but since returning for club and country in 2007 he is still rightly regarded as one of the world's best.

PROFILE
Born: Plzen, Czechoslovakia, May 1982
Clubs: Blsany, Sparta Prague, Rennes, Chelsea
International: Czech Republic

PEPE REINA

BORN to be a goalkeeper, Pepe Reina is part of the golden generation of Spanish number-ones.

The son of famous Barcelona and Atletico Madrid keeper Miguel Reina, Pepe followed in his father's footsteps by starting out at the Nou Camp.

A move to Villarreal followed before a big-money switch to Liverpool in 2005 as manager Rafa Benitez put his faith in his fellow countryman.

His judgement was immediately vindicated as Reina revived the tradition of top-class goalkeepers at Anfield and helped Liverpool win the FA Cup in his first season, while also setting a club record of 11 successive clean sheets.

Renowned as a specialist at saving penalties, Reina got the better of Chelsea in the Champions League semi-finals in 2007 to repeat his father's appearance in the final of the European Cup, although both ended up as losers.

In March 2009 Reina kept his 100th clean sheet for the Reds and although he has been unable to usurp Iker Casillas as Spain's first-choice goalkeeper he collected a winner's medal in the 2008 European Championships.

PROFILE
Born: Madrid, Spain, August 1982
Clubs: Barcelona, Villarreal, Liverpool
International: Spain

Champions League Trivia

Wembley has hosted the Champions League final five times and will do so again in 2011.

Barcelona's final win over Manchester United in 2009 takes Spain clear of Italy as the most prolific winners of the Champions League with five successes. England remains on three wins since the Champions League format started in 1992/93.

According to UEFA, the gross income for the 2008/09 Champions League competition was expected to be 820.5m Euros (around £700m) with 585.6m Euros going to the clubs involved from the group stages onwards. Winners Barcelona pocketed seven million Euros.

No-one has ever scored a hat-trick in a Champions League final, although the feat was achieved twice in the European Cup by Ferenc Puskas (Real Madrid 1962) and Pierino Prati (AC Milan 1969).

Manchester United's defeat in the final in Rome was their first in the 2008/09 competition.

The fastest goal ever scored in the Champions League took just 10.03 seconds from kick-off and was scored by Roy Makaay of Bayern Munich against Real Madrid in 2006.

Seven teams have won the Champions League with an unbeaten record right through from the group stages, including Manchester United in 2008 and 1999.

Cesc Fabregas and Aaron Ramsey were both just 17 when they scored their first goals in the Champions League for Arsenal but they are not the youngest ever scorers in the competition. That is Peter Ofori-Quaye who was 17 years, 195 days when he netted for Rosenborg in 1997.

Only two coaches have won the Champions League or European Cup with two different clubs. Ottmar Hitzfeld did it with Borussia Dortmund in 1997 and Bayern Munich in 2001. Ernst Happel was successful with Feyenoord in 1970 and Hamburg SV in 1983.

The most goals scored in a Champions League match is 11 from an 8-3 win by AS Monaco against Deportivo La Coruna in 1983.

ARSENAL
OUT-GUNNED

ARSENAL'S wait for a trophy extended to four years following a blank in 2008/09 but Arsene Wenger's men gave it a real go in the Champions League and were just one game away from a second final appearance in three years.

The European title continues to elude the Gunners but again they were a major part of the Premier League's four-pronged challenge until great rivals Manchester United scuppered their hopes of a final re-match with Barcelona.

Despite being held to a goalless draw at home to Fenerbahçe, Arsenal made smooth progress through the group stage with stand-out results in the return game in Turkey and at home to Porto when the Gunners rattled in a total of nine goals in two games.

Qualification was ensured by Nicklas Bendtner's late goal against Dynamo Kiev at the Emirates Stadium in the penultimate game, although top spot was ceded to Porto when a young Gunners side lost 2-0 in Portugal.

That meant a last-16 tie against AS Roma, which Arsenal negotiated in a dramatic penalty shoot-out.

A spot-kick converted by Robin van Persie gave Wenger's side the advantage from the first leg after Kolo Toure and William Gallas's dawdle out of the dressing room forced Arsenal to start the second half at the Emirates with just nine men.

Roma levelled early in the return through Juan and the Italians then missed a number of other chances as the tie went to a shoot-out. Eduardo missed for the Gunners but Manuel Almunia saved from Mirko Vucinic and after Abou Diaby had scored in sudden death Max Tonetto blazed over to send Arsenal through.

Villarreal waited in the quarter-finals but were no match for the Londoners who sunk the Yellow Submarines in clinical style.

A superb overhead kick from Emmanuel Adebayor earned Arsenal a 1-1 draw in Spain and they then finished the job at the Emirates with a superb 3-0 win.

A clinical finish from Theo Walcott and another from Adebayor killed off Villarreal and Van Persie added the third from the penalty spot as Arsenal reached the semi-finals for the second time.

Old foes Manchester United then stood in Arsenal's way of a trip to Rome and even though United won the first leg 1-0 at Old Trafford thanks to John O'Shea's goal there looked to be everything to play for in the return leg.

The Emirates Stadium was rocking in anticipation of an Arsenal onslaught but instead it all fell flat as an early slip from defender Kieran Gibbs allowed Ji-Sung Park to strike early.

And when Cristiano Ronaldo beat Almunia with a long-range free-kick it was effectively game over.

Ronaldo added a brilliant third on the counter-attack and Van Persie's late penalty, awarded after Darren Fletcher was dismissed for a foul on Cesc Fabregas, was of little consolation as Arsenal saw their dream die for another year.

Tartan Torment

SCOTLAND'S challenge in the 2008/09 Champions League barely got out of first gear in a disappointing year for the Old Firm.

Rangers' bid was over even before the Scottish Premier League season kicked off as they were shock victims to Lithuanian side FBK Kaunas in the second qualifying round.

Kaunas were beaten 4-1 on their last visit to Ibrox eight years previously but this time they hung on to secure a 0-0 draw in the first leg as Rangers were made to pay for missed chances.

And their worst fears were then realised when Walter Smith's side, which had reached the final of the UEFA Cup in 2008, lost 2-1 in the return leg to crash out.

Kevin Thompson put Rangers ahead and despite an equaliser from Nerijus Radzius the Scots were set to go through on away goals until Linas Pilibaitis headed in a corner four minutes from the end to seal the upset.

As SPL champions, Celtic went straight into the group stages but after progressing to the last 16 in the two previous seasons they couldn't make it a hat-trick.

Goals were to prove elusive and that was Celtic's undoing in their Group E opener against Aalborg BK who left Celtic Park with a 0-0 draw after Barry Robson saw his penalty saved.

Having never won an away game in the Champions League, Celtic maintained that unwanted record with defeats at Villarreal and Manchester United to stay on the back foot.

A late goal from Ryan Giggs for holders United then denied Celtic a win in the return after Scott McDonald had scored for Gordon Strachan's men to all but end their hopes of making the last-16.

And the consolation of a place in the UEFA Cup was then taken away with a 2-1 defeat to Aalborg in Denmark.

Celtic led through Robson but two deflected goals summed up the Scots' campaign as they were consigned to bottom spot.

A closing 2-0 win over ten-man Villarreal, secured with goals from Shaun Maloney and Aiden McGeady, salvaged some pride but with no European football in Scotland beyond Christmas the Old Firm were left to slug it out over domestic matters.

Champions League

WORDSEARCH

SOLUTION ON PAGE 61

```
M  F  X  R  C  H  E  L  S  E  A  G
D  E  T  I  N  U  L  P  Y  T  M  K
A  R  S  E  N  A  L  T  R  I  S  L
W  Y  L  S  J  R  L  O  A  N  N  I
C  E  L  T  I  C  M  X  F  I  O  V
Y  T  T  C  X  E  Y  E  E  E  I  E
L  E  W  D  T  H  U  D  U  S  P  R
J  G  N  T  P  G  N  L  N  T  M  P
Y  H  H  O  A  G  R  M  L  A  A  O
L  L  R  E  O  T  Q  B  K  Z  H  O
B  T  L  K  R  R  Q  M  J  Y  C  L
R  F  B  A  R  C  E  L  O  N  A  R
```

CHAMPIONS	ROME	CHELSEA
LEAGUE	UNITED	LIVERPOOL
BARCELONA	ROONEY	ARSENAL
MESSI	UEFA	CELTIC
INIESTA	TROPHY	

SUPERSTARS
OF EUROPE

ANDRES INIESTA

THE SPANISH maestro has been a star at Barcelona since emerging through the club's youth system and scaled new heights in a golden 12 months culminating in Barça's triumph in the 2008/09 Champions League final.

Lionel Messi grabbed many of the headlines following Barcelona's 2-0 win over Manchester United, but to many Iniesta was the outstanding player on the pitch.

A creative midfield player who never gives the ball away, the Spain international had also broken Chelsea's hearts in the semi-finals when his last-gasp goal at Stamford Bridge sent the Blues crashing out.

Having clocked up 250 games for Barcelona, Iniesta then drove the Catalans on to complete a second double of Champions League and La Liga titles in the space of three years.

His contribution to Spain's 2008 European Championship success also earned him a place in the team of the tournament and furthered his claim to be firmly ranked among the best players in the world.

PROFILE
Born: Fuentealbilla, Spain, May 1984
Clubs: Barcelona
Position: Midfield
International: Spain

THEO WALCOTT

A RISING star of British football, Theo Walcott has the world at his feet with both England and Arsenal.

A lightning-fast forward, Walcott has been carefully nurtured by Gunners boss Arsene Wenger since he snapped him up from Southampton for £5 million in 2006.

Soon afterwards the youngster was a surprise selection in Sven Goran Eriksson's World Cup squad for the finals in Germany.

That proved a false dawn but with increasingly regular starts for Arsenal his outstanding potential is now being realised as a creator and scorer of outstanding goals.

In September 2008 Walcott became the youngest England player to score a hat-trick when he led Fabio Capello's side to a crucial World Cup qualifying win in Croatia.

And even though his efforts could not help Arsenal past the semi-finals of the Champions League in 2009, the biggest stage surely awaits him.

PROFILE
Born: London, March 1989
Clubs: Southampton, Arsenal
Position: Forward
International: England

FRANK LAMPARD

AT CLUB level, English football has produced few better players than Frank Lampard.

An inspirational force in Chelsea's midfield, Lampard has been one of the main ingredients of the Londoners' success in the Roman Abramovich era.

After perfecting his trade and earning his first England caps while at West Ham, Lampard moved across London in 2001 and has barely missed a game since.

During his time at Stamford Bridge he has won every domestic trophy and helped Chelsea reach the final of the Champions League in 2008, where he scored in a losing cause against Manchester United.

No midfielder has ever scored more goals for Chelsea and as well as the quantity and quality of his strikes, it is often the importance of his goals that stand Lampard out as a great player.

That was perfectly illustrated in Chelsea's thrilling Champions league quarter-final against Liverpool in 2009 when the Reds stood on the verge of a major upset before Lampard's clinically taken late goal calmed the nerves and took Chelsea through.

PROFILE
Born: Romford, June 1978
Clubs: West Ham, Chelsea
Position: Midfielder
International: England

DIEGO FORLAN

WHEN Diego Forlan left Manchester United in 2004 as an unfulfilled talent, few would have expected him to go on and become one of the most feared strikers in Europe.

But thanks to prolific spells in Spain with Villarreal and Atletico Madrid that's what the Uruguay international has become.

It took Forlan 27 games to break his goal-scoring

luck as a United player and although he left with a Premier League winners' medal he scored just ten goals in all during two years at Old Trafford.

But after moving to Spain he never looked back. In his first season at Villarreal his 25 goals made him the country's top-scorer and joint winner of the European Golden Boot with Thierry Henry as the Yellow Submarines qualified for the Champions League for the first time.

Forlan scored more than 50 goals at better than one every two games for Villarreal before taking his finishing skills to Madrid where the goal glut continued.

In 2008/09 Forlan bagged a remarkable 32 goals in 33 games as Atletico Madrid finished fourth in La Liga and earned another crack at Champions League qualification, while Forlan again walked away with the Golden Boot.

PROFILE
Born: Montevideo, Uruguay, May 1979
Clubs: Independiente, Manchester United, Villarreal, Atletico Madrid
Position: Striker
International: Uruguay

Liverpool Feeling the Blues

LIVERPOOL'S record in European football is unmatched in British football but hopes of a sixth European crown were dashed by old foes Chelsea in one of the all-time great Champions League matches.

The two Premier League rivals keep on clashing on the European stage with both enjoying famous semi-final wins in recent seasons.

In 2008/09 they met one round earlier but served up a game at Stamford Bridge worthy of any final before Rafa Benitez's boys crashed out to concentrate on their brave effort to catch Manchester United for the domestic title.

Benitez has forged a reputation as a European specialist during his time

at Anfield and the Reds breezed through their Group D campaign, topping their group with an unbeaten record.

Atletico Madrid were their chief rivals as the teams traded 1-1 draws. Robbie Keane scored one of his few Liverpool goals in Spain before a late Steven Gerrard penalty rescued a point in the return at Anfield.

Gerrard's header then guaranteed a last-16 place for the fifth year running before goals from Ryan Babel, Albert Riera and David N'Gog at PSV Eindhoven guaranteed top spot.

The result was a glamour tie against Spanish giants Real Madrid in the first knock-out round and Liverpool responded with one of their finest European performances.

A late header from Yossi Benayoun gave Liverpool a famous win at the Bernabeau Stadium and then at a rocking Anfield the Reds romped to a 4-0 win.

Fernando Torres opened the scoring and with Real all at sea against an inspired attacking display, Gerrard doubled the lead from the spot.

The inspirational Reds captain grabbed his second with a thumping goal after the break before Andrea Dossena got a late fourth to cap a magical night.

The result sent shock-waves around Europe but Liverpool's elation was punctured in their quarter-final first leg against Chelsea.

Chelsea had found Anfield a fortress on their recent European visits but this time they stormed the barricades with a 3-1 win.

Torres gave Liverpool the lead but slack marking allowed Branislav Ivanovic to twice head home from corners and a third from Didier Drogba looked to have put the tie out of Liverpool's reach.

Liverpool refused to accept their fate, though, and in the second leg at Stamford Bridge almost pulled off one of the competition's great upsets.

A cunning free-kick from Fábio Aurélio and a Xabi Alonso penalty put the Reds 2-0 up at half-time.

And even though Chelsea roared back with goals from Drogba, Alex and Frank Lampard, Liverpool weren't finished.

Lucas scored with a deflected shot and when Dirk Kuyt headed in Liverpool were back in front on the night and one away goal from going through.

On an incredible night there was another goal to come but sadly for Liverpool it came from Lampard a minute from the end as Chelsea, rather than the Reds, marched on.

FIRST AND LAST FOR
Shakhtar Donetsk

SHAKHTAR DONETSK brought the curtain down on the UEFA Cup by becoming the first club from Ukraine to win a European trophy since the country gained independence in 1991.

Shakhtar beat German side Werder Bremen 2-1 after extra-time in the final in Istanbul.

They became the 25th-different winners of the competition which was first won by Tottenham in 1972 but which has been replaced from the 2009/10 season by the new-look Europa League.

Luiz Adriano put Shakhtar ahead and although Naldo equalised for Werder Bremen, the heavy Brazilian influence in the Shakhtar line-up paid off when Jadson turned in a cross from Darijo Srna for the decisive goal.

The home challenge was led by Manchester City, who came closest to becoming the seventh

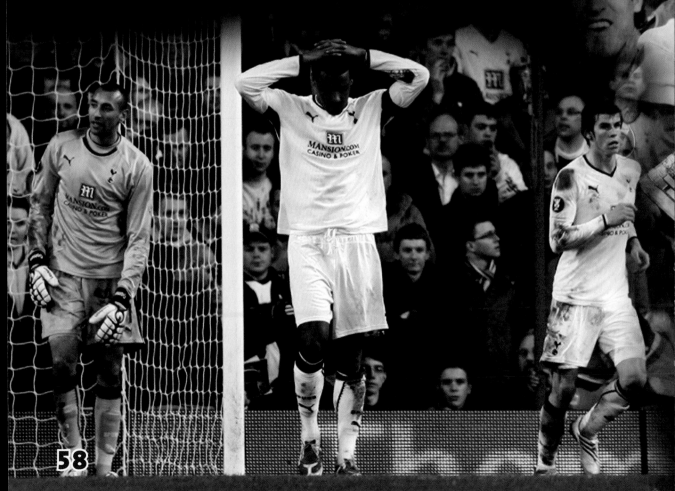

British winner, following on from Liverpool (2001, 1976, 1973), Tottenham (1984, 1972) and Ipswich Town (1981).

Everton and Motherwell went out in the first round, while Portsmouth fell at the group stage.

Aston Villa and Tottenham were knocked out in the last-32 but City went all the way to the quarter-finals before losing a thrilling tie 4-3 on aggregate to Martin Jol's Hamburg.

UEFA CUP WINNERS

2008 – 2009 Shakhtar Donetsk
2007 - 2008 FC Zenit St. Petersburg
2006 - 2007 Sevilla FC
2005 - 2006 Sevilla FC
2004 - 2005 PFC CSKA Moskva
2003 - 2004 Valencia CF
2002 - 2003 FC Porto
2001 - 2002 Feyenoord
2000 - 2001 Liverpool FC
1999 - 2000 Galatasaray AŞ
1998 - 1999 Parma FC
1997 - 1998 FC Internazionale Milano
1996 - 1997 FC Schalke 04
1995 - 1996 FC Bayern München
1994 - 1995 Parma FC
1993 - 1994 FC Internazionale Milano
1992 - 1993 Juventus
1991 - 1992 AFC Ajax
1990 - 1991 FC Internazionale Milano
1989 - 1990 Juventus
1988 - 1989 SSC Napoli
1987 - 1988 Bayer 04 Leverkusen
1986 - 1987 IFK Göteborg
1985 - 1986 Real Madrid CF
1984 - 1985 Real Madrid CF
1983 - 1984 Tottenham Hotspur FC
1982 - 1983 RSC Anderlecht
1981 - 1982 IFK Göteborg
1980 - 1981 Ipswich Town FC
1979 - 1980 Eintracht Frankfurt
1978 - 1979 VfL Borussia Mönchengladbach
1977 - 1978 PSV Eindhoven
1976 - 1977 Juventus
1975 - 1976 Liverpool FC
1974 - 1975 VfL Borussia Mönchengladbach
1973 - 1974 Feyenoord
1972 - 1973 Liverpool FC
1971 - 1972 Tottenham Hotspur FC

WORDSEARCH SOLUTION

M	F	X	R	C	H	E	L	S	E	A	G
D	E	T	I	N	U	L	P	Y	T	M	K
A	R	S	E	N	A	L	T	R	I	S	L
W	Y	L	S	J	R	L	O	A	N	N	I
C	E	L	T	I	C	M	X	F	I	O	V
Y	T	T	C	X	E	Y	E	E	E	I	E
L	E	W	D	T	H	U	D	U	S	P	R
J	G	N	T	P	G	N	L	N	T	M	P
Y	H	H	O	A	G	R	M	L	A	A	O
L	L	R	E	O	T	Q	B	K	Z	H	O
B	T	L	K	R	R	Q	M	J	Y	C	L
R	F	B	A	R	C	E	L	O	N	A	R

MAZE SOLUTION

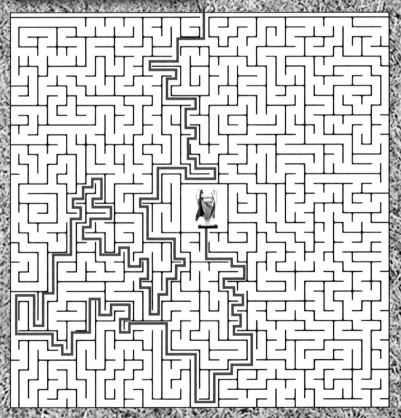

QUIZ ANSWERS

1 Cameroon

2 Three

3 Guus Hiddink

4 Bernabeu Stadium, Madrid

5 AC Milan - seven

6 Romania

7 Darren Fletcher

8 Chelsea 7 Liverpool 5

9 Celtic

10 Steven Gerrard

11 Barcelona

12 Carles Puyol